NAME
YOUR
BLESSING

Insight for Wise Parents

GREG RICHARDSON

NEWMAN SPRINGS PUBLISHING
320 Broad Street
Red Bank, NJ 07701

First originally published by Newman Springs Publishing 2019

ISBN 978-1-64531-470-7 (Paperback)
ISBN 978-1-64531-471-4 (Digital)

Printed in the United States of America

To all the parents
who realize the importance of investing in their child's future.

CONTENTS

Section III

INTRODUCTION

Everyone has a name. Most people have a vague idea what their name means, but few give their name considerable thought (Campbell 2019; Nuessel 1992). A name is very important. There are many name books, and a large number of them provide the meanings of names. People use name books to get names for their newborn children. A name is so important that God gives guidelines about His name to men in the third commandment. He says, "You shall not take the name of the Lord your God in vain, for the Lord will not hold him guiltless who takes His name in vain" (Ex. 20:7 New King James Version).

The Bible indicates that there are good names, and implies that some are not so good (Pro. 22:1; Ecc. 7:1). Reflectively, a good name has value similar to monetary wealth. Hearing such phrases as "making a name for himself" or "made a name for himself," people think of someone's accomplishments, present or past. Seldom is there an association to the individual's mannerism (Richardson 2002). Some people make that connection; they align the person's accomplishments to previously observed behaviors. Those behaviors made the person noteworthy of recognition. From that point, people say that particular individual has a good name or bad name.

Knowing the meaning of one's name is close in importance to insight about one's family lineage. Such knowledge gives an individual a greater sense of value, pride, and purpose. Discovering the meaning of one's names—first, middle, and last—is an important aspect to learning more about one's self. While several books exist on names and their meanings, the key information presented in this book is not an attempt to discredit, disprove, or dismiss another's research on names.

This book gives greater detail to the importance of knowing that all names have meaning, provides insight into unusual names, and addresses the true purpose and power of a name. This book explains how and why personality is embedded in a person's compiled names. This book consists of three parts. Section I thoroughly defines a name, provides foundations for ascribing names, discusses naming practices, and gives an overview of naming patterns. Section II of the book explains how names tell a story, addresses name(s) relation to character, and affirms the alignment of given names to one's personality. Section III describes various decoding processes, speaks to constructing baby names, and provides concluding insights on naming your blessing, your wonderful baby, that precious new member to your family.

Several terms used in this book enhance clarity for a better understanding on names. Definitions of these key terms are as follows:

Character	The set of qualities that make somebody, especially somebody's qualities of mind and feelings (Soukhanov 2001, X).
Diagraph	A union of two successive letters representing one sound (Soukhanov 2001, X), as in *ey, ph,* and *sh.*
Etymology	The study of the origins of words or parts of words and how they have arrived at their current form and meaning (Soukhanov 2001, X).
Gematria	The association of number to letters in words to determine the meaning (Blech & Blech, 1999).
Morphology	The branch of linguistics that deals with words, their internal structure, and how they are formed (Aronoff & Fudeman 2011, 2).
Morpheme	The minimal unit of grammatical analysis; the unit of meaning in one segment of a word (Lyons 1977, 181).

Onomastics	The study of proper names, their origins, and their formation (Soukhanov 2001, X).
Personality	The totality of somebody's attitudes, behavioral patterns, and emotional responses, plus traits that endure over long periods (Soukhanov 2001, X).
Prefix	A linguistic element that is attached to the beginning of a word to modify its meaning (Soukhanov 2001, X).
Semasiology	The branch of linguistic semantics that studies word meanings and the development of words (Soukhanov 2001).
Suffix	An ending affixed to the end of an existing name with no modification (Nuessel 1992, 61).

SECTION I

NAMES

What Is a Name?

A name is a specific label with a categorical function. Hence, a name is often a noun that functions as an identifier of a person, as well as a place, a thing, an event, or an idea. A name is the distinctive designator of a person who has particular attributes. Frequently, a name is a verb; it is "the vessel that carries hopes and dreams from parents" to the child (I. Sakamoto, peer faculty member, in discussion with the author, September 2, 2010). Subsequently, a name designates current or future behavioral characteristics of an individual.

A name is a personal possession that can bring insecurity, obscurity, blame, shame, or fame. People who consider their identifier a valued possession tend to cherish their name. Some are often quick to tell others how to pronounce their name, even when spelled incorrectly, phonetically. Occasionally, a name engenders positional power and authority. Such is the case when a representative acts on behalf of a king or governmental agency.

A name is an intangible asset. For instance, Shakespeare's Juliet Capulet in her love discourse with Romeo (a member of a warring family) asked him to denounce his father's name (Montague), saying to him, "What's in a name" (Hankins 1960)? Then she tells Romeo, "It is your name that is my enemy" (Hankins 1960). However, in this instance, Romeo's name was a deficit to his relationship with Juliet. Yes, one's name has a direct bearing on present and future relationships. Research indicates that people's names speak into their success

(Lansky, 2014; Wolfe, 2011). Subsequently, a high probability exists that names are audible windows of a person's life path.

A name is a hopeful aspiration for an individual. A name is a future expectation or belief obvious to the name givers. A name is a personal desire of the self-pronounced name bearer.

Understanding Names

Purpose. Everyone has a purpose for their existence which goes beyond eating, sleeping, and dying. As Isaiah the prophet proclaims, "The Lord hath called me…from the bowels of my mother hath He made mention of my name" (Isa. 49:1 NKJV). Life's purpose is all too often harmoniously demonstrated in one's profession, personality, and name. Subsequently, a name has three purposes. A name distinguishes one person from another. Two, name declares the reason for one's existence. Three, a name impacts one's future behavioral characteristics.

Onomastics. Every name has an associated meaning, whether intentional or unintentional. The term associated with understanding names is *onomasiology*, which asks for the identification of an entity's name (Blech & Blech 1999). The field of onomasiology touches upon the disciplines of linguistics, history, anthropology, and sociology (Campbell 2019; Mayrand 2018). Mayrand (2018) indicates in his article, *Origins and Meaning of Names,* that the study of onomastics covers the how, where, origin, and diverse spelling of names. As he posits, there is much more to name development than it may appear.

Von Markheim's (2017) insight on name meaning proceeds even further. In an article entitled *Names (Onomastics): How to Do Name Consultation,* he declares that names are definitive of personality. In essence, he says that a name cloaks the bearer's personality. While popular opinion may not align with such understanding, the more precise term that relates to personality embodiment in names is the study of semasiology. Semasiology is the branch of linguistic semantics that studies word meanings (Soukhanov 2001). Semasiology begins with a specific word (or name) and then asks, *What does the word mean?* The foundation of every name has a significant bearing on its meaning, and its meaning is a major factor that impacts the bearer's personality.

FOUNDATIONS FOR
ASCRIBING NAMES

Early Linguistics

The attention that names solicited with the ancient Greeks resurfaced during the twentieth century (Summerell 1995; Van Langendonck 2008). The fascination with names continues to astound linguists, anthroponomastics, and many others. Historical accounts of the formation of continents, nations, languages, words, and letters are essential in understanding names.

Biblical Relevance. Before the existence and dominance of three specific kingdoms of the world—the Babylonians, the Medio-Persians, and the Greeks—the Bible recorded God historically saying, "Here they are, one people with a single language" (Gen. 11:6 New English Bible). God gave credence to the strength of people uniting for a specific purpose; their spirit of oneness enabled impossibilities to materialize. The unfavorable project, the tower of Babel, was the inauguration of multiple languages (Gen. 11:7). It was from that location that "The Lord scattered (people) abroad from there over the face of all the earth" (Gen. 11:9 NKJV). From one body of land, called Pangea, the earth separated (global tectonics) into different continents (Dalziel 1995; Roy 1999; Torsvik & Cocks 2016). The biblical record further stated, "to Eber were born two sons; the name of one was Peleg: for in his days the earth was divided" (Gen. 10:25; 1 Chr. 1:19 NKJV). Appropriately, the name Peleg means division (Unger 2006).

The Alphabet. Early communication eventually necessitated a medium for long-distance messaging to articulate a speaker's thoughts. Subsequently, an early form of writing resulted from the formation of graphic symbols. Logan (2004) declared that spoken word depictions were either symbolic (ideograms) or pictorial (pictograms). Today, the evolution of these graphic symbols is called letters, and the complete group of letters an alphabet, which "is not the only form of writing" (Logan 2004, 4).

The first alphabet system consisted of twenty-two letters and was invented by the Semitics (Canaanites) 3,500 years ago (Logan 2004; Petrariu 2013). This alphabet was the model used for many national languages, including English. Logan (2004) explained that the English alphabet, with roots tracing back to the "Etruscan, Greek and Phoenician alphabets," was derived from the Roman alphabet (3). Greek reform of the Semitic alphabet incorporated vowels which allowed sound representation in writing (Logan 2004; Petrariu 2013). Interestingly, "vowels have a greater importance in phonology and also in morphological relationships...where the vowel gradation might indicate a difference in time or aspect for verbs" (Petrariu 2013, 195). Words exude sounds as morphemes embody meanings. Earlier alphabetic principles demonstrated the invisible and active power contained in words (names).

Early Writings

According to Logan (2004), all writing systems are not alphabets. Origination of writing preceded the origination of the alphabet by hundreds of years (Senner 1991) with the northern Semitic alphabet recognized as the oldest (Allot 2000). Allot (2000) posits that this articulatory alphabet of diagrams constitutes characters formed by combining representations of various speech organs. The alphabet of the ancient Chinese and Hebrews is a pictographic script. In the Paleo-Hebrew script, each letter is a word picture that has meaning (Seekins 2011). Compiled letters (word pictures) constitute compound meanings, several thoughts united. When individual letters are linked the collective becomes a word, which also has a meaning. The collection of several words form a sentence of thoughts that tell a short story. The grouping of multiple thoughts (sentences) constructs a paragraph. A paragraph is a larger detailed narrative.

Naming Practices

Names are diverse and originate from such sources as parents, circumstances, occupations (Mayrand 2018). Geographical events or other justification items associated with the selection processes of names are indicative of the historical naming patterns. The time and locale of the origin of a naming practice are as significant to understand names as time and locale are to the termination of the naming practice.

Historical References

Personal observations revealed that some names were purposeful duplications of the father's first name, an aunt's request, or the parents' phonetic choice. For some people, name pronouncement existed because of something the name bearer regularly did. The joy or the pain a parent experienced at the time of the child's birth prompted particular names. Such things as flowers, consumer products, circumstances, or events may prompt parents to select a particular child's name. Consider these Biblical incidents:

> Then Rachel said, 'With great wrestlings I have wrestled with my sister, *and* indeed I have prevailed." So she called his name Naphtali. (Gen. 30:8 NKJV)

And the child grew, and she brought him to Pharaoh's daughter, and he became her son. So she called his name Moses, saying, 'Because I drew him out of the water. (Gen. 2:10 NKJV)

Now his daughter-in-law, Phinehas' wife was with child, *due* to be delivered; and when she heard the news that the ark of God was captured, and that her father-in-law and her husband were dead, she bowed herself and gave birth, for her labor pains came upon her. And about the time of her death the women who stood by her said to her, 'Do not fear, for you have borne a son.' But she did not answer, nor did she regard it. Then she named the child Ichabod, saying, "'The glory has departed from Israel!' because the ark of God had been captured and because of her father-in-law and her husband. (1 Sam. 4:19–21 NKJV)

At the time of my birth, my mother was a beautician. She allowed her two adolescent customers to dictate both my first and middle names. So name choices come from diverse sources.

Name Selecting

People are influenced by multiple things when it comes to naming their child, such as current practices, accepted customs, or the race and religion of the parents (Nuessel 1992). Twenge and Manis argued that "names are one of the first things we learn about people," and according to Henning (1995) and Campbell (2019), naming customs vary greatly. The best naming practices and the best names constructed are pleasing to the ear, are pronounceable, and are unique (von Markheim 2017). Nonexistent rules govern the spelling and pronouncing of names (von Markheim 2017). It is the prerogative of the person who selected the audible identifier to pronounce it outside of formal phonetic conventions. Nevertheless, all names have significance.

Parents. After parents give the gift of life (procreate), the next gift usually bestowed upon the child is a name. This patronymic and matronymic duty places the parent in the role of a prophet (Blech & Blech 1999). The prophet is the individual who pronounces blessings upon people. If parents know the meaning of a particular name that they like, it is a natural tendency to hope for a future for the child that the name implies.

Names often reveal a parent's educational level and their child's destiny (Twenge & Manis 1998). Nevertheless, parents from both high socialeconomic and low socialeconomic strata customize formulation of names for their baby. There is no discovered evidence as to why this practice exists. Blech and Blech (1999) posit, according to tradition, naming a child after someone makes the original namesake the guardian angel, the protector, or an interceder on high. Blech and Blech continued by providing naming examples of Sephardic Jews—Jews from Spain, Portugal, Italy, North Africa, or the Middle East—who customarily name children after their beloved who are still living. Then there were the Ashkenazi Jews—Jews from Central or Eastern Europe—who name their children after deceased or perpetuated relatives (Blech & Blech 1999; Nuessel 1992).

An expectation is what some parents have in mind when they name their child. There exists a parental hope that their child lives up to what the child knows their name to mean. By labeling, parents distinguish their child from the masses (Chamary 2010). Nevertheless, the presumed power attributed to the crowning of a name on someone is as prophetic as it is reverential.

Culture. While the practice of calling something by an identifier is a state of normalcy, continual controversy exists over naming practices. Most cultures have some form of a naming practice (Henning 1995; Wamitila 1999). A naming practice is synonymous with naming pattern. The naming pattern could consist of the given name, the middle name, and the family name (Henning, 1995). The family name could have originated with one's occupation. Other naming patterns involve one to four elements (van Langendonck 2008). For instance, among some African countries, one name is the everyday name and the other name is the spirit-guarding name (Aceto 2002). Some countries (France, Germany, and Scandinavia), in avoidance of using unacceptable names, have official name lists (Henning 1995). In the West African nation of Ghana, due to the power embedded in names, parental choice in name selection of their children has been removed (Figlio 2005).

Family Traditions. Some families implement a creative naming practice. For instance, one family has six people in its family unit: the parents, a son, and three daughters. The first name of each family member begins with one of six sequential letters: I, J, K. L, M, and N. In another family, all the firstborn females carry for a middle name the first name of her mother. Reportedly, this practice is four generations deep. Another couple chose to give each of their seven children a Biblical name. The three boys were named after Old Testament prophets.

Naming Patterns

Personal Names

Mayrand (2018) posits that first (given) names come predominantly from five languages: Hebrew, Teutonic/Germanic, Greek, Latin, and Welsh. According to Henning (1995), the Norman Conquest started the practice of the first name taken from a Christian saint, hence the Christian name. Cultural addendums to given names are not limited to "family name (American), hometown's name (Polish), occupation name (English), husband's father's name (Brazilian), or mother's family name (Spanish)" (Henning 1995).

Ethnic Names

Most, if not all, Panamanians are known exclusively by their ethnic name(s), and "these ethnic names reflexively define who community members are regarding culture and ancestry" (Aceto 2002, 577). According to Aceto (2002), names used daily by these natives are their ethnic names, and names used by them in business are their legal names. Aceto further posits that "Ethnic names reveal characteristics of both nicknames and pseudonyms" and "often indicate the creation of a new social identity" (586, 584).

Uncommon Names

According to Nuessel (1992), some ethnic groups place unusual names on others "from the perspective of the majority group" (p. 4). Most ethnic names are uncommon name variants and often lead to negative self-evaluations, unfavorable reactions by others, and attribute to increases in school dropout rates (Ellis & Beechley 2012; Savage & Wells 2010; Twenge & Manis 1998). Uncommon names seem plagued with trouble (Figlio 2005; Bryner 2010). Research indicates that the name given to a child can cause problems or create opportunities well into adulthood (Bryner 2010). However, the belief in an unfavorable outcome relative to an uncommon name is contested by some (Zweigenhaft 2010).

How is it that some people with uncommon or unusual names succeeded in life? Twenge and Manis (1998) indicate that family is the variable that affects adjustment outcomes of children with uncommon names. One such individual is Barack Hussein Obama, the forty-fourth president of the United States, whose grandparents were great supporters (Scharnberg & Barker 2007). Whether a culture prompts an individual to use multiple names, nicknames, ethnic names, or uncommon names, it is essential that the researcher or wordsmith acquire an understanding of the foundation of names. Such insight is very helpful in decoding meaning from names.

Multiple Names

Early Romans during the Republic era ushering in the Principate period utilized only one name, until they followed the Chinese tradition by adopting three names. This three-part name—praenomen, nomen gentilicium, and cognomen—has significance. The praenomen, or forename, was the only one that parents could choose for their freeborn infant male Roman citizen. However, the key name for the Roman citizen was the nomen gentilicium which indicated the gens to which the male child was a member. The third name of the Roman male was the cognomen. The cognomen was the name used to address the Roman citizen and was also known as a nickname (Nephele 2003; Mayrand 2018).

Von Markheim (2017) purports, "Most people (were identified by a name) that consists of one given name plus one or two bynames" (IX.2.3). A byname was a broad term inclusive of surnames and derived for a variety of words (van Langendonck 2008). In a procedural explanation of byname selections around the globe, Mayrand (2018) explains that the Chinese were the first to adopt surnames (around 2852 BC) and their descriptive identifier consisted of only one syllable. Four millenniums later, during the twelfth century, the non-usage of a second name by many cultures was considered vulgar, and by the sixteenth century, family names gained popularity in Poland and Russia (Mayrand 2018, 3). Family membership usually determines the surname which is normally through birth or adoption. Mayrand (2008) also indicates that family names evolved from one or more four sources—parents, location, occupation (Henning 1995; Mayrand 2018), and personal characteristics—and that there exist multiple spelling variations. Mayrand further adds that Western Chinese people deviate from the Eastern tradition of placing the surname first.

Aceto (2002), author of *Ethnic Personal Names and Multiple Identities in Anglophone Caribbean Speech Communities in Latin America,* was able to determine how and when people identified themselves by a particular name. Aceto spent more than six months living among a Creole-speaking community in the Republic of Panama. His research addressed "the generation and maintenance of multiple personal names" used by the Creole-speaking community (577). Aceto discovered that names selected for use, either by that person or by someone else, were done so in the hope of positively impacting the future of the person identified by the name. If the chosen name did not to make a positive impact on one's future, then it was to make a positive impact on the public's perception of the person (Aceto 2002).

Nicknames

Aceto further states that the Panamanian alternative naming practice utilized nicknames. A nickname means different things to different people; nicknames "often indicate the emergence or creation of a new social identity" (Aceto 2002, 584). Aceto also states, "In the literature on naming and onomastics, any alternative name may ambiguously be labeled a nickname" (581). In an example, Corky was the nickname given to a particular individual when he was a child. At a particular stage in his younger life, he was known to expel gas frequently, hence the moniker Corky. In each preceding case, the individual's nickname was due to the repeated manifestation of particular observable behavior. Observed behavioral reliability seems to justify the placement of the nickname. Examples from penal system outreaches revealed that many men and women adopted names to define their characteristic to society: in and out incarceration. It was usually a name that they usually lived up to through osmosis or deliberate intentions.

Some researchers argued that a nickname, etymologically, was a "byname" or an "ethnic" name (Pulgram 1955; Aceto 2002). Not so. A nickname was usually attributed to an individual for some repetitive behavioral trait via the cultural lens of the society (Aceto 2002). In similarity to a nickname, a pet name tends to be an affectionate term attributed to a loved one.

Take the word *pseudonym* which is a composite of two Greek morphemes which mean "false name" (Aceto 2002). The precise translation is "assumed name" (Room, 1998). One, in some social science writing, a pseudonym cloaks the identity of a specific person. Two, the term pseudonym is considered a nickname as attribution to an individual because of identifying or behavioral characteristics. For example, Aceto (2002) indicates that the great jazz saxophonist Julian "Cannonball" Adderley did not receive his nickname from his massive size; he received it from his massive appetite. The alteration comes from *cannibal.*

Sometimes given names do not conform to any naming pattern. Asking several people how they got their name usually confirms this reality. However, in spite of the naming practice utilized, any name that uses the English alphabet is decodable. Even when a person's name is Westernized, such as changing Enrique to Henry, decipherability of the name to extract its meaning is still possible. Whether there is a name change, nickname, or pet name, the individual's personality hinges on the name answered to most.

SECTION II

STORYTELLING

Some individuals are people watchers. These individuals find people fascinating to watch. They visit shopping malls, amusement parks, or ballparks, tend to find a comfortable location, and observe people as they travel. Some of the things observed are appalling, and other things are quite comical. Each person visualized is telling one chapter from their personal story.

Consequently, most people, through osmosis, observe the habitual behavioral traits of other people, especially when they see them regularly. Whenever a particular behavior is repeated in an individual, appropriate or not, it's an attribute of the person's personality. In further validation, numerous participants in this nonexperimental pilot study on names acknowledged that they saw similar characteristics in people they knew who had the same name. Reportedly, "our name identifies who we are" (T. Roberts, civil rights activist, in discussion with the author, January 2018).

Words Tell a Story

Study of the basic elements of a word—etymology—validates the significance of earlier syllables; they contain a specific meaning. A group of letters combined make a word; a word is a short statement. Each word tells a story; each name tells a story. So, then, a short statement is a short story.

For instance, the word flood embeds a short story. The Chinese word for a *flood* is a compound word. As written, the word consists of the overlay of two words—water and eight. Both words carry an individual meaning. When these meanings compile, they tell a short story. The story speaks of great water, which gives reference to the flood, and the eight human survivors—Noah, his three sons, and each of their wives: eight people. In similitude, a compilation of meanings from each name (word) a person has tells a story.

Performative Utterance

A performative utterance accomplishes actions or creates a state of doings (AHDEL, 2010). A performative utterance is a declaration that functions as a bearer of performativity or illocution—the uttered effect (Doerge 2013). According to Dr. Marsha Fowler, senior fellow at Azusa Pacific University, "a performative utterance declares something that comes to pass" (M. Fowler, professor of spirituality and ethics, in discussion with the author, March 2011). In essence, a performative utterance enunciates a futuristic action or event according to its meaning (obvious or subliminal) relative to a specific statement or spoken word. The phenomenon of a performative utterance applies to names, as well.

An excellent example of a performative utterance occurred in Genesis 1:1, the first book of the Bible. The creation account, according to Blech and Blech (1999), profoundly indicated that "When the Torah (Bible) said that 'God created' it did not suggest that (God) worked or that He fashioned through labor, but merely that He said—and the very words described the object made it come into being" (p. 3). Blech and Blech purport that spoken words create tangibles. The act of naming by God made words key catalysts in the creation process. Blech and Blech (1999) further said, "Names are responsible for the differences between all things on this earth" (p. 3). Names are the predictive nature of every entity, especially humans. Words are creative forces that penetrate the environment. United into a statement, these words are often called positive statements or affirmations. Details in the following section explain further how words and names impact one's environment.

Names and Their Meanings

People of Arabic, Asian, or Indian ethnicity and whose ancestry originates across either the Atlantic or the Pacific Ocean often know the meaning of their given name. These individuals usually accept the meaning of their name as their identity, their destiny, and as a key aspiration in life. That aspiration all too often becomes a self-motivating goal.

Possessing knowledge that names have meaning is informational. For instance, connotation components embedded in the name Wang, which is Chinese, means yellow. The name Drukker is Dutch and means one who prints, whereas the name Yale means a dweller at a secret place. Multiple African societies have proverbial sayings that indicate that the name defines the child (Wamitila 1999). The concept that proper names are connotative is not arbitrarily accepted (Lyons 2012; van Langendonck 2008). This book explains how names contain meaning.

Allan (2014) reported that all language makes sense because language asks the question, *What is the meaning?* But proper names do not ask that question. Some researchers argued that a name is only an identifier or signifier to distinguish one individual from another, and that a name does not contain meaning or make sense (Algeo 1973; van Langendonck 2008). In concurrence with van Langendonck (2008), the question is not whether names have meaning; it is in "what way the meanings (of names) are construed and function" (38). The set of rules used to govern language, which consists of word combinations, enables each fraction of language to have meaning (Allan 2014). Since all names have a referent; the problem then is the discovery of the referent (or its meaning) by way of a proven decoding method. The decoding method determines the rules.

Names Tell a Story

Mill, the nineteenth-century British philosopher, could not refute the assertion that names describe the person because no record exists that he successfully deciphered names. Nonetheless, names are words that tell a story; they tell the story about a specific person. The name of a person is allegorical to a book about the person. The book's contents are readable and subjective to observable interpretation. According to Blech and Blech (1999), a name: (1) tells a story, (2) captures a person's character and personality, and (3) defines a person (ix, 5). In essence, because every name tells a story, names are the embodiment of a person's personality. The Bible confirms this when it says, "As his name is, so is he" (1 Samuel 25:25 NKJV). Blech and Blech (1999) further indicate that the content in their book, *Your Name is Your Blessing,* is the inauguration of secrets from the Kabbalah. The Kabbalah is the body of ancient mystical biblical interpretation tradition wherein rabbinical origins unveil the significant power of a name as a unit of "prophecy and potential blessing" (Blech & Blech 1999, ix).

Furthermore, Blech and Blech (1999) make a profound statement that says, "Names Don't Just Name—They Create" (3). They allude to the concept that every name is an individual creative entity, an invisible creative force. The Bible in the Gospel of Saint John chapter 6 at verse 63 (NKJV) cites Jesus as saying, "The words that I speak to you are spirit, and they are life." One interpretation is that Jesus's words were invisible entities that give life to thoughts. John further says "The Word was with God" and "All things were made through Him" through the Word (John 1:1, 2 NKJV). This concept of words having the ability to initiate the very existence of an activity applies to names unequivocally.

Words that parents use to call their children seal the fate of their children, whether the child is young, middle-aged, or older. On October 17, 2001, the former talk show host Regis Philbin made a profound statement. He was interviewing Starlet Jones, co-host of the "The View." After commenting on Star's achievements, Regis said, "There's something in the name." Regis was accurate in his statement (Richardson 2002). Regis acknowledged that Starlet was a star, as her name so indicated. So it is with most people. People are, or tend to become, behaviorally, that which they are frequently called. Ren (2015) indicates that names start their influence early in life. As example, she says research that validates females near adulthood are less like to study certain STEM subjects if they have a traditional feminine name.

A name is a futuristic descriptor, a powerful entity (Henning, 1995; Aceto, 2002). Here are more examples that speak to name and behavior. Someone by the name of Stone might hear others say, "You are often insensitive and cold-hearted." Another person by the name of Joy may hear people say, "You are always positive, bubbly, and happy." In each scenario, the person seems to live up to the name, with obvious personality traits. A person's name(s) builds a foundation of potential accomplishments; names tell the story of an individual's future. People display characteristics of the name(s) used to identify them. There are two reasons why this occurs: (1) names are words, and all words have meaning; and (2) the meaning of a person's name, which is a word, affects their personality.

What then is a word? Aronoff and Fudeman (2011) define a word as the "smallest unit of syntax," and syntax is "the component of human grammar that governs the ordering of things" (35). Everything and everybody that God created has a specific purpose, a special functional order, designated for a slot in His divine plan. Names play a key role in identity and activity.

NAMES AND CHARACTER

Names of God

The Bible disguises the name of God by saying it "is a strong tower" (Pro. 18:10 NKJV). Thus, His name carries with it everything attributed to a tower of strength. The Bible also reaffirms that "(God's) name alone is excellent" (Psa. 148:13 NKJV). Nothing can be added to God's name to increase its worth, significance, power, or integrity (Richardson 2002).

A closer look reveals that God's name reflects his character. God's character defines His name. Each name of God is an identifier for Him, and it is His character. Matthew 6:9 says God's name is to be *hallowed*. Hallow means to honor as holy (righteous), to venerate (worship treating with respect), and to hallo (communicate with).

"For thus says the high and lofty One, who inhabits eternity, whose name is Holy" (Isa. 57:15 NKJV).

Any recipient of such exalted esteem must have the justifiable character. The character is God's, and so is the name—holy.

Have you ever wondered what God was precisely telling Moses when He told him that His name was *I am?*

> Then Moses said to God, "Indeed, *when* I come to the children of Israel, and say to them, 'the God of your fathers has sent me to you,' and they say to me, "What is His name? What shall I say to them?" And God said to Moses, *"I AM WHO I AM."* And He said, "Thus you shall say unto the

children of Israel, *'I am* has sent me to you.'" (Ex. 3:13, 14 NKJV)

GOD said to Moses that His name is His nature and His character. What He is called is *who He is.* God reemphasized His response to Moses's question by saying:

I Am that I Am	*I Am*
(Heb.—*I will be what I become*)	(Heb.—*I will be*)

To clarify further, God was saying that He (who inhabits past, present, and future)—makes the power (natural and spiritual), the creature (corruptible and incorruptible), the time (temporal and eternal)—*is* the source of existence for whatever is needed, desired, or provided. In retrospect, we are who we are (called) because God is who He is called (Richardson 2002).

Biblical Authors

Consider those biblical authors whose names end in—*el*, e.g., Samuel, Ezekiel, and Daniel. El is a derivative of Eloah (the Creator). Whenever *el* is exists in a name (front or back end), it means of God, by God, or from God. Before God sent out each author, a complete directive of his or her ministry's purpose was defined. Each biblical author's purpose was cleverly embedded in his or her name. Each syllabic part cloaked a meaning of the name. Once combined, these part revelations of their names were not mere coincidences, but divine destiny (Richardson 2002).

Other Biblical Names

The name of each character in the Old Testament revealed something astonishing. Each author's name was synonymous with his recorded ministry, as well as his character and personality. (Biblical author's names are usually defined in study Bibles in the *foreword section* of the particular book of the Bible.) The following are a few examples of those whose name meaning addressed their service to God. Ezra, whose name has the meaning of "help," was a priest. He confined himself mainly to events associated with the Temple to help people. Isaiah, "Jehovah Saves" by meaning, was married to a prophetess. And he foretold of the punishment the people who rejected God would receive if they did not accept God's salvation—he was also a mourner. Hosea, whose name means "deliverer," delivered a message of God's unchanging love in light of spousal unfaithfulness. Hosea felt God's pain, disgust, and anguish. He delivered love to his spouse but received pain. So his prophetic oration was with strong conviction, for he had firsthand insight into how God felt.

Name Alignment
to Personality

People call others by such names as Smarty Pants, Beautiful, and even Stupid. The reason behind such names varies on the observable traits. However, there are family names such as Smith, Perkins, and Dunn. It is quite interesting when people who do not know each other and who are from a different ethnic background display the same physical trait, such as shape of the earlobe or the same behavioral trait like head tilting. One explanation lies in genetics which is sometimes recognizable by the individual's last name. The preceding is one element of influence; additional effects exist in the other names of the person.

Personality and Behavior

A person's personality is linked to observed behavior and as Wamitila (1999) states, "a name...describes the object it names" (36). He further states that this concept is known as the sense theory of proper names. According to Aaker (1997), a person's personality is the result of multidimensional factors such as innate traits and behavior. Mayrand (2018) purports a person's name serves as a personal fingerprint in life. This claim is validated in the following statement:

> The (H)ebrew word for 'name' is שם shem. (Shem is a composite of) two (H)ebrew letters, ש shin and מ mem (that) are central to the word neshamah—נשמה—the Hebrew word for 'soul.' The soul, or essence, of any human is contained in his or her name. That is why if a person is critically ill, Jewish law suggests a powerful last resort to change the name of the individual in order to alter the decree. (Blech and Blech 1999, 4)

It is interesting that Jewish law authorizes name changes to alter a medical edict. As believed, the name change redirects the destiny of the person's health.

In Isaiah 1:5, God is recorded as saying, "Before I formed you in the womb I knew you." He knew our time of birth, the conditions of birth, our stature, and our ethnicity—God knew us. God knew of our physical, mental, and spiritual talents well before He developed them in us. God wrote the *owner's manual* that describes our capability and maintenance requirements.

God knows our operational design, intended function, service, and life span. He knows who and what we are fashioned to be—He is the designer. God tells us as He told Moses, "I know you by name" (Ex. 33:12, 17 NKJV). Names are indicative of a person's programmed contribution to society.

Positive Names. In some cases, a person had his name changed by an authoritarian who desired to augment the individual's destiny, e.g., Abram to Abraham (Gen. 17:5), Jacob to Israel (Gen. 32:28), Daniel to Belshazzar (Dan. 1:7), and Saul to Paul (Acts 13:9). For instance, Abraham's call from God entailed travel on a specific journey and a name change. The name change was similar to what a person experiences along life's journey, relative to when marriage occurs.

The name change affects the individual's purpose and the outcome. As an example:

> Then Abram fell on his face, and God talked with him, saying: "No longer shall your name shall be called Abram (Heb., the exalted father), but your name shall be Abraham (Heb., Father of a multitude); for I have made you a father of many nations." (Gen. 17:3, 5 NKJV)

Fatherhood for Abraham in his senior years meant exaltation, but it was not until the arrival of his promised son that Abraham was to become father of nations!

Although Ishmael (the legal-cultural son) procreated several nations, Isaac (the son of promise) also procreated several nations. Ishmael, by definition, means "God will hear" (Unger 2006). God heard the lad's voice in the wilderness and declared, "I will make (Ishmael) a great nation" (Gen. 21:17, 18 NKJV). Abraham's second son, Isaac, whose name means "laughter," also became a great nation (Unger 2006). Abraham (Gen. 17:17) and Sarah (Gen. 18:12) both laughed when they heard that God would bless Sarah to give birth to their son. However, God had the final laugh as Sarah and Abraham, now seniors, became parents. The descendants of Ishmael identified as Arabs and descendants of Isaac identified as Israelites are significant. It was the name change that enabled Abraham to become the patriarch whose sons fathered two great nations. Names can have either a positive or negative valence.

Negative Names. A man by the name of Nabal is an example of someone whose name has an unfavorable outcome. Nabal's behavior, a manifestation of his name, is mirrored in his name. According to the text, his behavior was a regular occurrence of inappropriate behavior.

> Please, let not my lord regard this scoundrel Nabal. For as is name is, so is he: Nabal is his

name, and folly is with him. (1 Sam. 25:25 NKJV)

Nabal's wife, Abigail, said her husband was *worthless*. By implication, Nabal was a stupid, mischievous, unprincipled, and miserable man. Abigail knew her husband because she spent plenty of time with him. Quora, which is a question-and-answer website created by Adam D'Angelo and Charlie Cheever, posted the question Why do some names have negative meanings? Linguistic Gassner replied in 2014 and linguistic Smith replied in 2015; both stated that an outward characteristic or a vocational duty was a common reason behind giving negative names. They posted two examples Cecilia, a blind person, and Travis, which meant a toll collector. However, even negative a name can yield positive outcomes when appropriately directed. In illustration, on an ordinal number scale, a negative two (-2) is greater in value than a negative seven (-7) and presents strong significance when value counts.

Nonetheless, life activities are contingent upon the meaning of the specific name. The irony is that the possessor of the name does *not* have to know what the name means to act out a particular character trait. The very articulation of the name attributed to a specific person resonates within the environment. The result is the definitive effect on the name bearer. Controversy exists on why or how audible sounds such as names impact personality, persona. However, the next section and the following chapter provide greater clarity.

Name Usage Frequency

Most people have several names such as a first name, a middle name, the last name, and maybe a pet name. While empirical data does not exist in the domain of a specific name's usage compared to the usage of another name, interviews and a decade of personal observations, reveal that personality attributes, personae, directly correspond to the overall percentage of each specific name used. The attributed identifier, one's name, and the frequency of its usage, unconsciously molds specific character traits within the person.

NAME TO PERSONALITY AFFIRMATION

Just as words create, personality is a creative by-product of an individual's name(s). A name is an audible sound released into the atmosphere. It vibrates and resonates with the bearer thereof and to everyone who hears that name. A name is an igniter of activity and a mandate of potential. This book outlines a new paradigm on name deciphering. The model uses the English alphabet to unveil personality embedded in the name(s). Today, controversy continues over the premise that such a task is possible. One reason is that many people do not want to believe that their actions and destiny are probable predictions based upon their name.

Destiny. Name pronouncement by the guardian directs the child's destiny, the child's purpose in life. Most parents have a desire to see their children succeed in life. Parents have a desire for their children to have a better quality of life than that which they did and during their child's life. This desire is articulated to children and on multiple occasions. Selected names define the mission of children. Every word that parents use to call their children helps to seal the fate of the child. Outcomes occur when the offspring are young, middle-aged, and even senior citizens. Parental proclamation is very powerful (Henning 1995). Each name a child has determines increases or decreases in personal resources—intellectually and monetarily. Subsequently, it is not uncommon to see parents bestow assets on their children in attempts to fulfill this innate parental obligation. Children become fortunate recipients of real estate, stocks and bonds, companies, and many other tangible and intangible assets. In actuality, name(s) are audible investments in the child's future which tend to become reality.

Personality Counterparts. Interpretations from a doppelganger provide valuable insight into names and their connection to personality. A *doppelganger* is an identifier given to people who see themselves (Cuthbert, 2008 2019; Owens 1987). Dr. David Drew, professor and former dean at Claremont Graduate University, shared a personal and interesting related experience. Here is the account as articulated by Dr. Drew:

> I received an email, I believe it was in 2000, and the person said that his name was also David Drew. He said that he saw two similarities between he and I and enclosed his resume. Upon my review of his resume, I noticed two more similarities that had to do with books. We corresponded more and even sent pictures of our families to one another. Later, I noticed some other similarities:
>
> 1. Our dissertations were longitudinal studies of college students.
> 2. Both of us taught statistics at the university level.
> 3. We have conducted policy research in our nation's capital.
> 4. Our most recent books were on how educational achievement as affected by ethnic, socioeconomic status.
> 5. Our most recent article is a statistical critique of the bell curve.
>
> (D. Drew, in discussion with
> author, February 2012)

The preceding doppelganger also provides a good scenario where a person's name and vocational pursuit coincide and it is another probable link to the association of a name to personality.

Relative to doppelganger is the term *implicit egotism* which was coined by Pelham, Mirenberg, and Jones (2002) in their article entitled *Why Susie Sells Seashells by the Seashore: Implicit Egotism and Major Life Decisions*. The implicit egotism concept, "suggests that people's positive automatic association about themselves…influences their feelings about almost anything that people associate(d) with (their) self" (Pelham et al., 2002). In essence, some people are motivated to migrate toward careers, people, things, and locations that remind them of their selves as a form of *unconscious self-enhancement*. In retrospect to the story involving Dr. Drew, the premise of implicit egotism is valid. Dr. Drew in England was drawn to locate and converse with Dr. Drew in America, and both individuals gravitated toward and actively worked in like careers with similar research interests.

Name Coincidences

I, too, am in education, and as interesting as this story is, a woman walked into my office the same day I had a visit with Dr. Drew. She said that she needed advising in her academic program. I commented on how unusual her name was. She immediately told that me that her mom made it up. Her name was Merruba (this is a pseudo) Smith. Then she told me that one day she decided to check Facebook to see if there were others with the same name. Merruba found six others with the same name—two males, and four females—and two of them had very similar interests. In consideration of these phenomena, one might ask the question, *How important is the construction of a name?* The construction of a name yields insight into understanding the name through deconstruction, deciphering.

Section III

DECODING NAMES

Extrapolating Names

Naming practices entail formation of letters to construct a name. Most names are compound entities that consist of a root and possibly a prefix and suffix. The meaning each definitive component of a name carries is the same meaning that component provides to any word that contains the same letter arrangement. Therefore, each fragment of a name has meaning and this impacts its compiled meaning of the name. Some people know what their name means but have difficulty believing that their given name influences their behavior, character, persona, and personal destiny. The key to gaining insight on name to personality is in decoding the individual's names.

Decoding Methods

Chen, Wenyin, and Zhang (2002), in using the Chinese language, attempted to decode names. In their article entitled *A New Statistical Approach to Personal Name Extraction*, the formula presented for decoding the meaning of names from graphic or phonetic composition was found lacking, and so was the Pinyin Research Model, which the article featured. The said model segmented names (which are words) into morphemic divisions for proper decoding. Although the article directs a person toward the interpretation of a personal name, it does so inadequately. The process required to decode names properly lies in understanding naming foundations, and then utilizing each decoded element of the word to determine the embedded message.

All personal names cannot be recorded or defined in a set of lexicons, and an accurate method of deciphering meaning is of great benefit. Proper decoding of a name is a requirement to extract the embedded meaning of a name fully. Since each name is a word, it has an affiliated word family. Therefore, it has a meaning. Names are words, and every word has a meaning. According to Henning (1995), "Names are invested with a power" (6). There exist various procedures to determine the unleashed power behind the meaning of a name. There exist numerous books that give the meaning of names. Name construction occurs under diverse methods, and meaning extraction necessitates a valid decoding process. Extraction of the meaning of a name is essential to explaining personality embodiment. This process constitutes having an understanding of gematria, morphemes, digraphs, and syllables.

Gematria. The first known method for decoding the meaning of a name lies in "the mathematical science of *gematria*—the calculation of numerical values of letters" (Blech & Blech, 1999). The science of gematria, the association of numbers to letters in words to determine meaning, is not widely known (Blech & Blech, 1999). Blech and Blech (1999) indicate that there are two kinds of gematria: perfect and simple. The first branch of gematria, the perfect, involves rearrangement of letters in one word to construct another; each word still has the same numerical value. According to Blech and Blech (1999), if a word has the numbers $2+3+5$ attributed to its three letters, there is "a deeper kinship" (7). That is, for at least two other words. Those words consist of the rearrangement of each letter, making the sequential number order $3+5+2$ or $5+2+3$. In each case, the total numerical value is 10. As an example, "the very word for *name* in Hebrew…has a gematria of 340 which, fascinatingly enough, is the exact (gematria) equivalent of the word…which means *book*" (Blech & Blech 1999, 7). The research of Blech and Blech (1999) indicates that gematria associates a name with the contents in a book. Have you ever heard the phrase, "I can read you like a book?" Such a statement also alludes to the predictive powers of one's name as an identifier of personality.

In a second example, the perfect gematria found in the Hebrew word for grave (קבר) has the letters for the words decay (ריקבון) and morning (בוקר) transposed; the provision of the exact numerical value exists once again (Blech & Blech 1999). Some biblical scholars may disagree with a specific connection or these words, or their numerical relevance in interpretation. The deduction is that the association of words (and their numerical equivalence) allude to the grave preceding decay, and decay preceding the biblical resurrection.

The Bible validates this premise when it says, "It is appointed unto men once to die but after this the judgment" (Heb. 9:27 King James Version). The second branch of gematria, the simple, identifies with the mystical tradition that links everyone's name to a specific numerical value in the Bible. Blech and Blech (1999) posit, "Every person has a biblical word linked to his or her name" and "it represents not simply what you are called, but your calling, your life's mission, and purpose" (9). While I do not fully concur with Blech and Blech that everyone has a comparative biblical name, I do agree that everyone's name represents their purpose for living.

Morphemes. Socrates, in his etymological investigation in Cratylus, placed words in semantic components he called *primary word* which were in all probability the precursors of morphemes (Allan 2014, 97). Morphemes are the smallest bearers of meaning in a word.

In linguistics, the study of the compound structure of words in a language is called morphology (Booji 2012; Freeman & Freeman 2014). An awareness of morphology is essential to understanding what a name means. Van Langendonck (2008) posits that the "basic level (of) meaning in proper names can be derived from their *morphosyntax*" (81)—morphemic and syntactic properties. Performance of this word segmentation is critical when it comes to construing the *authentic* meaning in a name.

The concept of Chen et al. (2002) goes beyond morphemes (the *micro* elements) to graphemes (the *macro* elements), which are null morphemes. Null morphemes are free of morphemic definitions; that is, they are without meaning. Chen et al. (2002) who use name (word) segmentation of Chinese Pinyin believes this would lead to a documented understanding of names written in the English language. Conversely, it did not. Pinyin is "a widely used method to input Chinese uses a typed string of phonetic letters and converts them into Chinese, using the best contextual word(s)" (Chen et al. 2002, Chinese Language Model and Pinyin Input, paragraph 1). Unfortunately, the article conveyed nothing about the meaning of any name converted or elements that construct or decipher the meaning of diverse components.

Diagraphs and Syllables. Digraphs and syllables are two- and three-letter sequels that produce a distinct sound. As a way of extracting meaning from these units, take a look at the syllable *re"* For instance, take people who have the letter combination such as *re* in their name—like *Re*nee, And*re,* or Andr*e*w. These individuals tend to be *repetitious* when it comes to particular actions. They often duplicate their behaviors, good and bad. Look closer at the name Renee. The *nee* of Renee insinuates fine probe capabilities. Definitive, Renee is a person who receives life again, a known replicator, one who penetrates unforeseen obstacles.

Furthermore, the *an'* found in Andre and Andrew implies *supplement,* while *dr'* means *fate endured.* When *and* is joined with *dre,* the full meaning of Andre defined is "an individual of sequel with repetitive endurance." The name Andrew has the same meaning and is more profound. The *w,* which means hook when added to *dre,* derives the meaning "hooked stamina." To clarify, the name Andrew means this is a person who not only has repetitive endurance but who also possesses an exponential capacity for stamina. Names conceal a type of invisible DNA that contains elements of character. Therefore, information from a person's name(s) reveals identity, personality, and probable life service.

CREATIVE NAME
CONSTRUCTION

Name Building

Methods that people use to construct new names are diverse. More diverse are some of the unusual spelling of names that surface. The following name examples carry the same phonetic sound but observe the difference in spelling: Geri, Gerry, Jerry. There exist numerous inspirational elements that prompt the conception of unique names, many accompanied with endless spelling constructions. Each name developed carries a significant message that its creators, parents or guardians, tend to recite periodically. The purposeful message usually centers on the propelling circumstances that existed during a specific time, event, or action. The structure of the name could exist because the parent likes the way the letters looked together. Nevertheless, every name has an extrapolated meaning. The name's meaning paves the way for personality development.

Literature validates that names have meanings, but methods used to arrive at a name's meaning are diverse and often unverifiable. Construction criterion—*etyma* (historical provision), *morphemes* (small meaningful units), *phonemes* (distinctive sounding units), *graphemes* (structural units), and human ideologies—influence the meaning of a given name. The structure of a name derives its associated meaning (Wamitila, 1999). In consideration of the vast number of names that exist, only a small pool of names have a clear, identifiable meaning, and there is no known scientific method in existence to construct or analyze a name other than the one proposed in this paper.

Von Markheim (2017) provides definitions of name-related terms, gives clarity to names, bynames, plus patronymic, matronymic, and diminutive names. Also, she makes a significant point when she asserts that, in essence, the embedded documented elements of a name have meaning which can be joined to produce another name. A person's name also consists of compound words (Henning, 1995; von Markheim, 2017) such as Mary Ann which carries a definition of both names. In a slightly different scenario, Henning (1995) said German and Celtic traditions used compound words for naming. The name Bald-win—"bold friend"—was provided as an example. Von Markheim (2017) mentioned that a "'new name,' whether invented by the submitter or borrowed from a literary source, (must) follow the same rules for name formation from a linguistic tradition" (IX.2.4). In many cases, a word may be a *loanword*—a word borrowed from another language.

> The history of words that have to do with loanwords, word formation, and sound symbolism is called etymology. The word itself come from ancient Athens (word) *etymologia*; *etymon* (true sense) + *logia* (study of) from *logos* (oration). Etymology makes use of philology (how words culturally change), comparative methods (parent language inferences), and root words. (Formentin 2008)

There are innumerable ways culture can structure a name (Henning, 1995). Most names are compound entities that consist of a root, and possibly a prefix and suffix.

Name Sectionals

The root of a name gives credence to the premise and existence of meaning embedded within the name. Wamitila (1999) indicated that names are codes, and that the decoding of names is not only possible but they are also highly important. Each fragment of a name has a meaning that impacts its synthetic meaning. The meaning that each component of a name carries is the same meaning that component provides to any word that contains the same letter arrangement.

NAME YOUR BLESSING

Insight for Your Child's Destiny

What is your blessing? Your blessing is your child's name with its embodied meanings. Your child's name is a statement of identity or destiny. Most parents desire for their children to succeed in life. They desire for their children to have brighter futures than they did, and during a child's life parents often communicate this desire to their children. For instance, parents bestow assets upon their children in attempts to fulfill this innate parental obligation. Thus, children are fortunate to become recipients of real estate, stocks, bonds, companies, and other assets. However, after the procreative gift of life, the first gift parents usually bestow upon their children is a name, and all names have significance. The pronouncement on a wrong or inappropriate name on a child sheds the risk on limiting potential, self-esteem, and other qualities in the child's future.

Anyone who has input into selecting or pronouncing a name upon a child should conduct some form of research before making a decision. Names influence the child's future and their relationship with others. All names have meaning, and all names come with personality traits. Regardless of the naming practices used, whether the name is prophetic or pathetic, the person who the name is pronounced upon ultimately is affected by that name. Even names that pronounce such attributes as virtue, integrity, strength, or leadership are worthy of research before attributing an identifying label to a child.

The recommendation is that the name givers research names to discover their meanings, especially since names are likely associated with personality. After all, the destiny of the child is in their hands, and the given names are key factors in the success of the child.

Receiving a Name Analysis

By now, you may want to analyze the chosen name(s) of your baby. Or perhaps you would like to have your name(s) or the name(s) of someone else analyzed. If the name you have in mind is unusual or has an unusual spelling, you have the right resource in hand to discover its meaning. If the person's name in mind is the same as that of a specific object, you have the right resource in hand to discover its meaning. If the name in mind is newly designed and consists of a unique spelling, you have the right resource in hand to discover its meaning.

By understanding your name or the name of someone else, you position yourself to enhance your relationship with others. More importantly, if the analysis is of a child, you can indirectly guide that child toward more success in life.

Research on the meaning of a particular name explores how that name may or may not reflect the course of one's life. As effective as our analysis proves to be, it is not failproof. Because of the many variables involved in personality development, along with the human subjectivity component in our name-to-meaning-to-personality analysis, pronounced results are not one hundred percent accurate. Nevertheless, our extrapolation and analysis results are excellent indicators of overall persona.

I encourage you to contact us to get your name(s) analyzed. Send an email to 2findyourname@gmail.com to acknowledge your interest and to receive for details.

BIBLIOGRAPHY

Aaker, Jennifer L. "Dimensions of Brand Personality." Journal of Marketing Research, 34, 347-356, 1997. doi. org.10.1177/002224379703400304

Aceto, Michael. "Ethnic Personal Names and Multiple Identities in Anglophone Caribbean Speech Communities in Latin America." Language in Society, 31, 577–608, 2002. doi:10.1017/S0047404502314040

Algeo, John. On Defining the Proper Name. Gainesville, FL: University of Florida Press, 1973.

Allan, Keith. Linguistic Meaning. New York, NY: Routledge, Taylor & Francis Group, 2014. doi: 10.4324/9781315880297

Allis, Oswald Thompson. Bible Numerics. Phillipsburg, NJ: Presbyterian and Reformed Publishing Co., 1974. Last updated December 5, 1998. http://www.christianbeliefs.org/articles/biblenumerics.html

Allot, Robin. "The Articulatory Basis of the Alphabet." In Becoming Loquens: More Studies in Language Origins, eds. Bernard H. Bichakjian, Tatiana Chernigovskaya, Adam Kendon and Anke Moller, 167–199. Frankfurt am Main, Germany: Peter Lang, 2000.

American Heritage Dictionary of the English Language (AHDEL), 4th ed. Boston, MA: Harcourt Publishing Company, 2010.

Anderson, John. M. "On the Grammatical Status of Names." Language 80(3), 435–474, 2004. doi.10.1353/lan.2004.0108

Aronoff, Mark and Kirsten Fudeman. What is Morphology?, 2nd ed. Chichester, West Sussex, UK: John Wiley & Sons Ltd, 2011.

Blech, Benjamin Rabbi, and Elaine Blech. Your Name is Your Blessing: Hebrew Names and Their Mystical Meanings. Northvale: Jason Aronson, Inc., 1999.

Booij, Geert. The Grammar of Words: An Introduction to Linguistic Morphology, 3rd ed. Oxford, England, UK: Oxford University Press, 2012.

Bryner, Jeanna. "Good or Bad, Baby Names Have Long-Lasting Effects." LiveScience, 2010. https://www.livescience.com/6569-good-bad-baby-names-long-lasting-effects.html

Campbell, Mike. Behind the Name: The Etymology and History of First Names, 1996. Last modified February 28, 2019. www.behindthename.com

Chamary, J. V. "The Name Game: how names spell success in life and love." Focus Magazine: Immediate Media Company, 2017. http://sciencefocus.com/feature/psychology/name-game

Chen, Zheng, Liu Wenyin, and Feng Zhang. A New Statistical Approach to Personal Name Extraction. San Francisco, CA: Morgan Kaufmann Publishers, Inc. International Conference on Machine Learning, 2, 67-74, 2002.

Cuthbert, Alan W. "Doppelganger." The Oxford Companion to the Body. Encyclopedia.com, 2019. Retrieved April 18, 2019. https://www.encyclopedia.com/medicine/encyclopedias-alamanacs-transcripts-and-maps/doppelganger

————. World of the Body: Doppelganger. New York, NY: Answers Corporation, 2008. Retrieved December 23, 2008. www.answers.com/topic/doppelganger

Dalziel, Ian W. D. "Earth before Pangaea." Scientific American Special Editions, 15(2), 14-21, 2005. doi:10.1038/scientificamerican0705-14sp

Doerge, Friedrich Christoph. "Performative Utterances." ResearchGate, 2013. https://www.researchgate.net/publication/260135043

Ellis, Albert, and Robert M. Beechley. "Emotional Disturbance in Children with Peculiar Given Names." The Journal of Genetic Psychology, 85, 337–339, 2012.

Figlio, David N. Names, Expectations and the Black-White Test Score Gap. NBER Working Papers 11195, National Bureau of Economic Research, Inc., March 2005. http://www.nber.org/papers/w11195

Formentin, R. "Etymology." Answers.com, 2008. New York, NY: Answer Corporation. www.answers.com.

Freeman, David E., and Yvonne S. Freeman. Essential Linguistics: What You Need to Know to Teach Reading, ESL, Spelling, Phonics, and Grammar, 2nd ed. Portsmouth, NH: Heinemann, 2014.

Hankins, John Erskine, ed. The Tragedy of Romeo and Juliet. New York, NY: Penguin Books, 1960.

Henning, Jeffrey. Model Languages, 1(3), July 1, 1995. Last modified March 1996. http://www.datapacrat.com/True/LANG/JAHENN~1/ML0103A.HTM

Houghton Mifflin Harcourt Publishing Company. "The American Heritage Dictionary Entry." American Heritage Dictionary—Search, 2018. Accessed April 06, 2018. http://ahdictionary.com

Lansky, Bruce. 2015. 100,000+ Baby Names: The Most Helpful, Complete, and Up-to-Date Name Book. New York, NY: Hachette Books, 2014.

Logan, Robert K. The Alphabet Effect: A Media Ecology Understanding of Western Civilization. Cresskill, NJ: Hampton Press, 2004.

Logan, Robert K. The alphabet effect: A media ecology understanding of the making of western civilization. Cresskill, NJ: Hampton Press, 2004. http://openresearch.ocadu.ca/id/eprint/1585/

Lyons, John. Introduction to Theoretical Linguistics. Cambridge, England, UK: Cambridge University Press, 1968. Published online June 2012. doi.org/10.1017/CBO9781139165570

———. Semantics. Vol. 1. Cambridge, England, UK: Cambridge University Press, 1977.

Mayrand, Lionel E. "Origins and Meaning of Names." Mayrand. Org, n.d. Accessed December 18, 2018. www.mayrand.org/meaning-e.htm

Mill, John Stuart. A System of Logic: Being a Connected View of the Principles of Evidence and the Methods of Scientific Investigation: in Two Volumes. London, Great Britain: Longmans, 1875.

Nuessel, Frank H. The Study of Names: A Guide to the Principles and Topics. Westport, CT: Greenwood Press, 1992.

Pelham, Brent W., Matthew C. Mirenberg, and John T. Jones. "Why Susie Sells Seashells by the Seashore: Implicit Egotism and Major Life Decisions." Journal of Personality and Social Psychology, 82(4), 469–487, 2002. doi:10.1037//0022-3514.82.4.469

Petrariu, Iulia. "Greeks, Phoenicians and the Alphabet." Studia Antiqua et Archaeologica 19(1): 189–197, 2013.

Pulgram, Ernst. Theory of Names. Potsdam, NY: American Name Society, 1955.

Ren, Jenny. "What's in a Name?: How Our Names Affect Our Lives." Catalyst: Rice Undergraduate Science Research Journal, November 16, 2015. http://ricecatalyst.org/discoveries/names

Richardson, Greg. When the Shoe Fits: How to Discover Your Ministry. Houston, TX: Messiah Books, 2002.

Room, Adrian. A Dictionary of Pseudonyms and Their Origins, with Stories of Name Changes. 3rd ed. Jefferson, NC: McFarland & Company, Inc., 1998.

Roy, A. B. "Assembly and Breakup of Supercontinents: A Story of the Changing Map Patterns of the Earth." Resonance 4(7): 42-48, July 1999.

Savage, B. M., and F. L. Wells. "A Note on Singularity in Given Names." The Journal of Social Psychology 27(2): 271–271, 2010. doi.org/10.1080/00224545.1948.9918930

Scharnberg, Kristen, and Kim Barker. "The not-so-simple story of Barack Obama's youth." Chicago Tribune, 25, March 2007.

Seekins, Frank T. Hebrew Word Pictures: How Does the Hebrew Alphabet Reveal Prophetic Truth? Scottsdale, AZ: Hebrew World Inc., Hebrew Heart Media, 1999.

Senner, Wayne, ed. The Origins of Writing. Lincoln, NE: University of Nebraska Press, 1991.

Shakespeare, William, and John Erskine Hankins. The Tragedy of Romeo and Juliet. Chennai, Tamil Nadu, India: MJP Publishers, 2017.

Soukhanov, Anne H. Microsoft Encarta College Dictionary: The First Dictionary For the Internet Age. New York, NY: St. Martin's Press, 2001.

Summerell, Orrin F. "Philosophy of Proper Names. In Names Studies, 1, 368–372. Charlottesville, VA: University of Virginia Press, 1995.

Torsvik, Trond H., and L. Robin M. Cocks. Earth History and Paleogeography. Cambridge, UK: Cambridge University Press, 2016.

Twenge, Jean, and Melvin Manis. "First-Name Desirability and Adjustment: Self-Satisfaction, Others' Ratings, and Family Background." Journal Applied Social Psychology 28(1), 41–51, 1998. doi: 10.1111/j.1559-1816.1998.tb01652.x

Unger, Merrill F. The New Unger's Bible Dictionary, edited by R. K. Harrison. Chicago, IL: Moody Publishers, 2006.

van Langendonck, Willy. "Theory and Typology of Proper Names." In Trends in Linguistics: Studies and Monographs 168, eds. Walter Bisang, Hans Henrich Hock, and Werner Winter, xvi+378, 2008. New York, NY: Mouton de Gruyter.

von Markheim, Alison. "How to Do Name Consultation." West Kingdom College of Heralds, August 1986. Last modified on November 2017. http://heralds.westkingdom.org/Handbook/vi_2-HowToDoNameConsultation.thm

Wamitila, Kyallo Wadi. "What's in a Name: Towards Literary Onomastics in Kiswahili Literature." AAP 60, 35–44, 1999.

Wolfe, M. "Does Your Name Spell Success?" AOL Jobs Contributor. Last modified January 2011. Accessed April 06, 2019. http://www.aol.com/2009/02/02/does-your-name-spell-success

Zweigenhaft, Richard L. "The Other Side of Unusual First Names." The Journal of Social Psychology 103(2): 291–302, 1977. Published online July 1, 2010. doi.org/10.1080/00224545.1977.9713328

ABOUT THE AUTHOR

Greg Richardson is a former engineer and professor. He is also a minister who has served nationally and abroad. He has publications in both Christian and educational areas. His most recent article publication, *Faith and Learning in Higher Education: Merging the Bible with Discipline-specific Content,* is in press.

Inspiration for *Name Your Blessing* came to Greg while studying the Bible. During one particular study on I Samuel chapter 25, he noticed what Abigail said to David about her abrasive and dishonest husband, Nabal:

"Please, let not my lord regard this scoundrel Nabal. For as his name *is,* so is he: Nabal *is* his name, and folly *is* with him (NKJV)!"

The man was a fool. Nabal acted foolishly by withholding provisions from King David's men during their travels. This deliberate suppression led to Nabal's pending fatality. Fortunately, his wife intervened. By further critical thinking, Greg saw the association of name to personality.

Reportedly, Greg then began to think about one of the given names of Jesus—Immanuel—which, in Hebrew, means God with us (Isa. 7:14; Mat. 1:22). Believing that God incarnated as a man, Greg deduced that letters of the English alphabet that spelled the name *Im-man-u-el* would extrapolate to mean *I'm-man-god.* This deduction partially confirms his hypothesis since *el* meant "god" to ancient Semite and Canaanite cultures.

Further research by Greg revealed that biblical names—Daniel, Ezekiel, Michael, and Samuel—had meaning and were descriptive of the individual's personality and, in some cases, their service to

God. Greg received additional insight from God on how to extrapolate meaning from names written or pronounced phonetically with the English alphabet. Also, pilot studies confirmed extrapolation of name meaning accuracy, as well as its personality association.

CPSIA information can be obtained
at www.ICGtesting.com
Printed in the USA
LVHW041215101120
671255LV00001B/68

9 781645 314707